ANTS

Consulting Editor: Fredric L. Frye, DVM; MS; Fellow,
Royal Society of Medicine

The title of the Spanish edition is *El fascinante mundo de
las hormigas*

All inquiries should be addressed to:
Barron's Educational Series, Inc.
250 Wireless Boulevard
Hauppauge, New York 11788

Library of Congress Catalog Card No. 91-15664

International Standard Book No. 0-8120-4721-4

Library of Congress Cataloging-in-Publication Data

Julivert, Angels.
    [Fascinante mundo de las hormigas. English]
    The fascinating world of ants / by Angels Julivert :
illustrations by Marcel Socías
        p. cm.
    Translation of: El fascinante mundo de las hormigas.
    Summary: Describes the appearance, life cycle,
activities, and social habits of ants.
    ISBN 0-8120-4721-4
    1. Ants—Juvenile literature. [1. Ants.] I. Socias,
Marcel, ill. II. Title
QL568.F7J8513   1991
595.79'6—dc20
                                    91-15664
                                        CIP
                                        AC

Printed in Spain
4   987654

THE FASCINATING WORLD OF...

ANTS

by

Angels Julivert

Illustrations by Marcel Socías

BARRON'S

ANTS IN THE WORLD

There are a great many varieties of ants in the world—more than 12,000 species—all very different in appearance and behavior.

These little insects are found throughout the world, from high mountains to deserts.

Ants are *social insects* like bees, and belong to the order of hymenoptera. They live in colonies formed by thousands of ants that work in teams to assure the community's survival. Therefore, they must be able to communicate with each other. They transmit messages by means of chemicals, by scents, and by touch.

The ant's body, like all insects' bodies, is divided into:

■ **The head**, usually large, is where the sense organs (sight, smell, and touch) are found.

■ **The thorax** has six legs attached to it. Some species also have two pairs of wings, but most ants lack them.

■ **The abdomen** is linked to the thorax by means of a thin waist.

■ **The legs**. Ants support themselves and walk on three pairs of jointed legs.

Right: Anthill of black ants in full activity.

Below: There are two groups of ants: The **stinging ant**, which is characterized by its sting and a peduncle (the joint between the thorax and the abdomen) that is formed by two pieces; the **red ant** which has no sting and its peduncle is formed by a single piece.

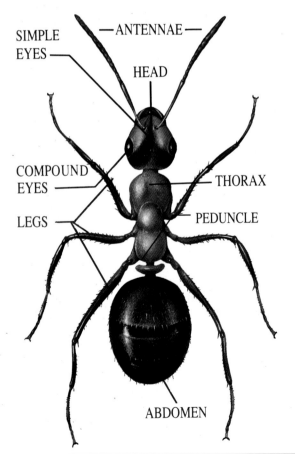

SIMPLE EYES

—ANTENNAE—

HEAD

COMPOUND EYES

THORAX

LEGS

PEDUNCLE

ABDOMEN

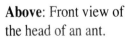

Above: Front view of the head of an ant.

Left: Parts of the anatomy of an ant.

STINGING ANT

RED ANT

THE INHABITANTS OF THE ANTHILL

Three different kinds of ants live in the anthill: one or several **queens**, the **males**, and a large number of **workers**.

The queen is the largest ant in the colony and her function is to lay eggs. She is born with four wings but loses them after her nuptial flight. Her life is quite long—she can live 10, 15, or, depending on the species, more than 20 years.

The workers are very numerous and are wingless. They are responsible for all the nest tasks. All are female, but they cannot lay eggs. Sometimes they travel far away from the nest to search for food. Many species leave a scent to help them find their way back to the colony. The sun's position also helps them to orient themselves.

In certain periods of the year, males appear in the nest. They always have wings. Their only purpose is to fertilize the future queen and then they die.

In some species, queens, males, and workers are similar, but most of the time they are quite different from each other.

Right: The most active ants are the workers. Here we see them in the central chamber, attending the queen ①, and entering an adjacent chamber occupied by a male ②.

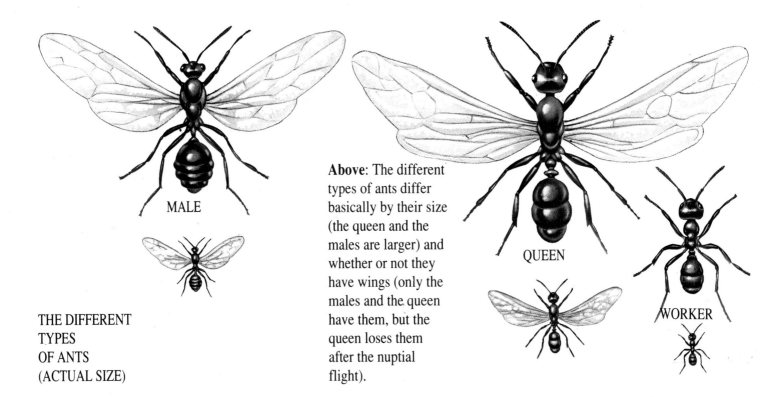

MALE

THE DIFFERENT TYPES OF ANTS (ACTUAL SIZE)

Above: The different types of ants differ basically by their size (the queen and the males are larger) and whether or not they have wings (only the males and the queen have them, but the queen loses them after the nuptial flight).

QUEEN

WORKER

THE BUSY WORKERS

The workers are always very busy, whether inside or outside the nest. Some of them gather food for the entire colony. Others clean, repair, and guard the anthill. The youngest ones usually take care of the queen and her young.

Sometimes workers in the same nest differ in size and shape—from small worker ants to larger soldier ants. These differences do not exist in all species. Some species have only one kind of worker.

The soldiers are large workers with huge heads and highly developed, powerful jaws. They are in charge of the defense of the anthill, but they also carry out other tasks. There is one species whose soldiers block the entrance to the nest with their big heads and prevent invasion by strangers. When an ant of the colony wants to enter, it touches the soldier's head with its antennae. These unusual guards recognize their worker companions by their smell and let them in.

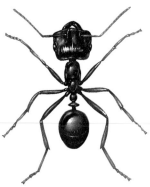

LARGER SOLDIER

ORDINARY SOLDIER

MEDIUM WORKER

SMALL WORKER

Left: Comparative study of workers' sizes. Note the size of the head of the soldiers.

Below: A soldier protects the nest, which has been dug into a trunk, by blocking the entrance with its huge head. A worker identifies itself by touching the soldier's head with its antennae.

Right: The workers' activity is constant: They carry grain ①, put it in the store-house ②, feed the queen in her chamber ③, and take care of the larvae ④.

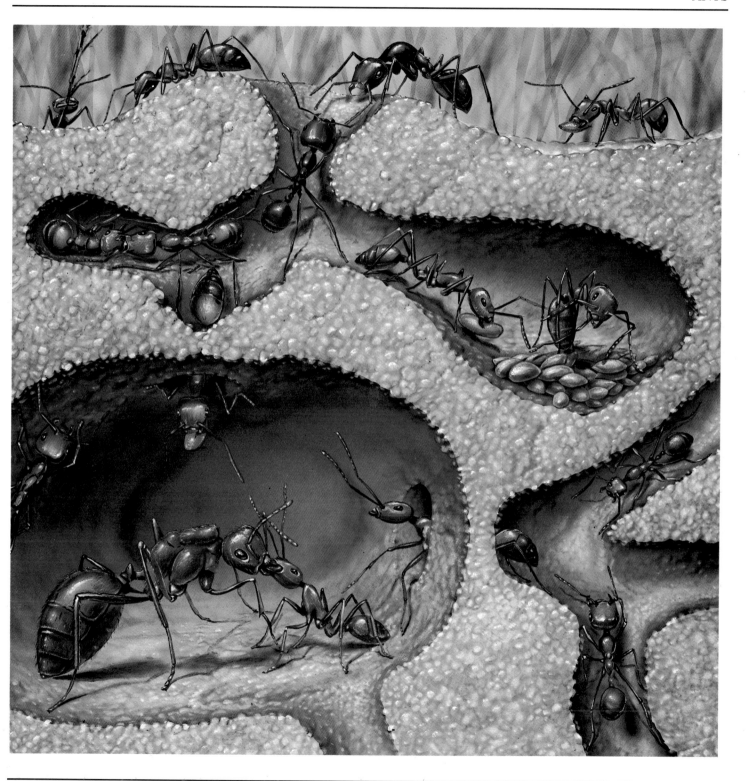

FROM EGG TO ADULT

T he queen lays a large number of **eggs**. There are two kinds of eggs: *fertilized eggs*, that will hatch into female ants (workers or queens) and *unfertilized eggs*, that will become male ants.

The workers move the little eggs to special chambers and clean and moisten them constantly with their saliva. Within a few days the **larvae** are born. They have no legs and need a great deal of food. They are very different from adults.

As they grow, the larvae change (or molt) their skin several times until their development is complete. After the last molt, they become **nymphs**.

At this stage, most of them weave a silk cocoon that protects them. They are the so-called **"ant eggs"** that are sold to feed fish.

During this period the developing ants do not feed and the workers move them to other chambers which are drier and warmer to help their development.

Little by little their bodies change and when their **metamorphosis** is complete, they will emerge as adults.

Some larvae do not make these cocoons. They remain unprotected during the nymph stage.

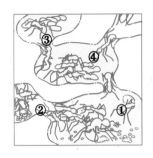

Right: Anthill of the stinging group:
① The queen's chamber, where she is laying eggs.
② Egg chamber.
③ Cocoon's chamber.
④ Nymph's chamber.

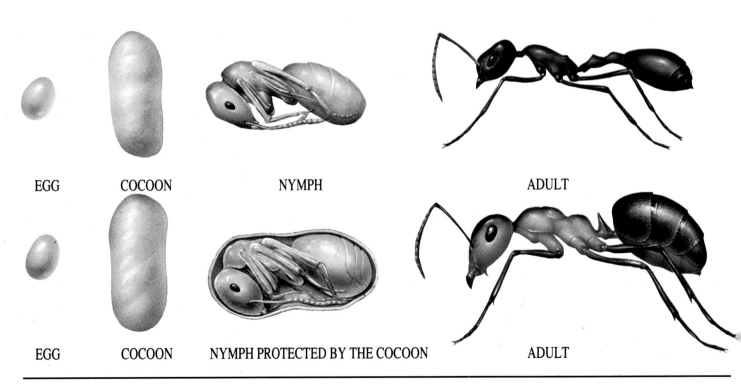

| EGG | COCOON | NYMPH | ADULT |

| EGG | COCOON | NYMPH PROTECTED BY THE COCOON | ADULT |

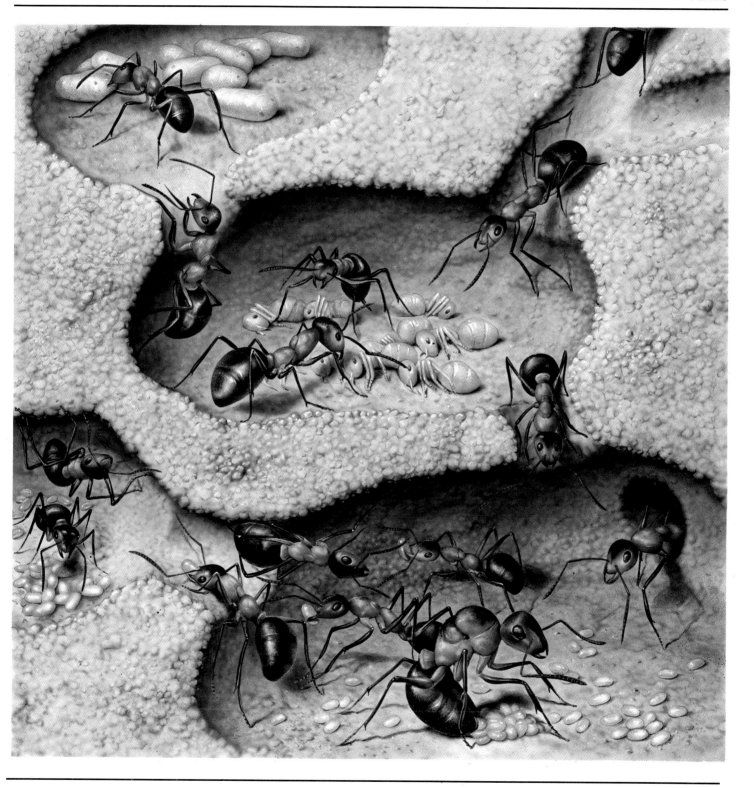

THE ANTS' DWELLING

The anthill is formed by a network of tunnels and passages dug in all directions, with numerous chambers of different sizes and at different levels.

Some of these chambers serve as storehouses; others are nurseries for the young. There are often little passages connected to the outside to ventilate the dwelling.

The nests the ants build may have many different shapes and sizes, according to the species. They connect with the outside through one or several exits.

The usual anthill is an underground nest that can extend several feet in depth. It can contain a great many inhabitants. In spring the ants clean the passages. The small mound of soil that forms around the entrance gives a clue to their presence.

MOUND OF THE RED ANT

The *red ant*, which lives in forests, builds large anthills with a central area dug underground and a large mound outside made up of withered leaves, small twigs, and vegetable remains, which are carefully woven together. The entire nest is provided with many tunnels.

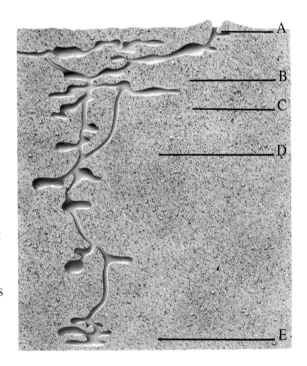

Right: Cross section of an anthill of the stinging group. It shows the tunnels and chambers.

Above: Large mound formed by twigs and leaves at the entrance to a nest of red ants. Sunlight warms the mound, thus raising the temperature inside the nest.

Right: In an underground anthill there is a main entrance (A), although it may have several ventilation tunnels. The grain storehouses (B and C) are spread throughout the anthill. There are several unused tunnels (D); chambers for breeding (E) are placed at the deepest levels.

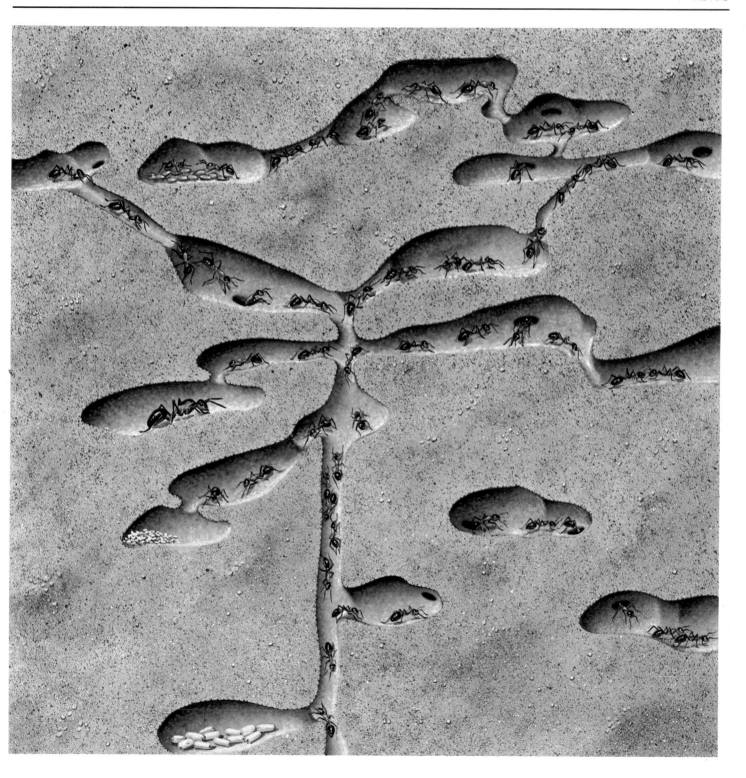

SKILLFUL SPINNERS

Spinner ants construct very special nests by connecting one tree leaf to another with silk threads woven by their larvae.

A group of workers grasp the edge of a leaf with their legs and then reach for the edge of another leaf that they secure with their jaws. Then they pull both ends together to connect them.

If the leaves are wide apart, the workers form a chain, fastening on to each other until they reach their objective. Other workers take the larvae in their jaws and move them from one leaf to another until the leaves are connected. In this way the larvae serve as tiny glue dispensers.

Little by little, the leaves are connected and the nest is built, hanging from the branches like a huge cocoon. As the colony grows, the ants constantly mend and enlarge the nest.

Other species prefer to make their nests inside tree trunks. **Carpenter ants** make tunnels in old trunks, piercing and chewing the wood with their strong jaws.

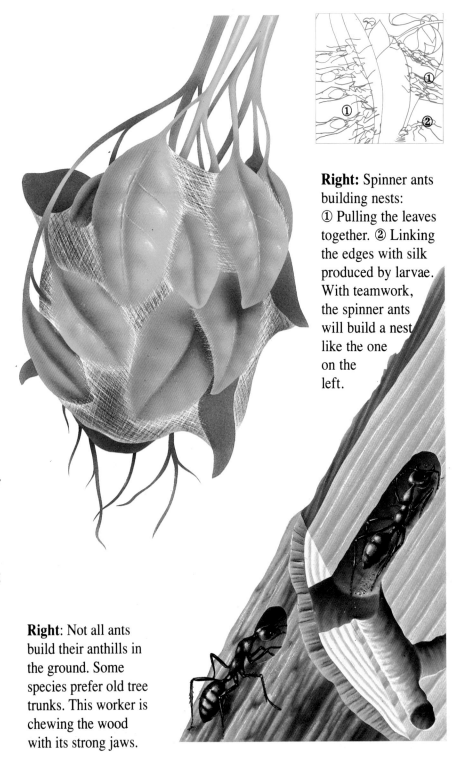

Right: Spinner ants building nests: ① Pulling the leaves together. ② Linking the edges with silk produced by larvae. With teamwork, the spinner ants will build a nest like the one on the left.

Right: Not all ants build their anthills in the ground. Some species prefer old tree trunks. This worker is chewing the wood with its strong jaws.

A NEW FAMILY

When spring arrives, many winged ants appear in the colony. They are the males and the future queens who leave the nest and start the nuptial flight.

Sometimes they form very large swarms, since they leave all the nests in the same area at the same time.

Every queen mates with one or several males who fertilize her. Shortly after, the males, having accomplished their mission, die.

The young queen then establishes her own colony. She sheds her wings and searches for a hiding place to lay her first eggs.

In the beginning, she is alone and must care for and feed her young. She does not go in search of food, feeding on the reserves contained in her now useless flight muscles and also on some of the eggs.

Soon the first workers are born and free their mother from her domestic tasks. The colony grows quickly and the workers continually enlarge the nest.

MATING OF A MALE AND A QUEEN

But the establishment of a new family is not always done this way. In some species the queen is accompanied by workers who will help her. Other times, several queens gather together and start a new colony.

Left: After their nuptial flight, the queens are fertilized by one or several males and lose their wings.

Right: Once fertilized, the young queen leaves the anthill and looks for a place to set up her nest, as the one in the upper part of the illustration is doing. When she finds the right place, she lays eggs and the development of a new colony begins.

Left: The presence of many winged ants means the beginning of the nuptial flight.

SHARING THE ANTHILL

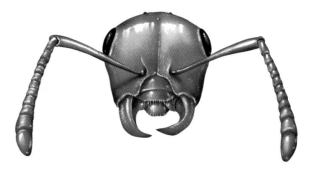

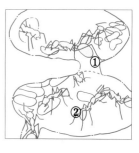

U sually all the inhabitants in the anthill belong to the same species. But sometimes, mixed colonies are formed where two different species share the same nest.

One of the species benefits from the other one, which does all the work.

The Amazon ants, as they are called in some countries, are not capable of obtaining food, and they depend completely on the workers of other species.

They attack other ants' nests in large groups and move the oldest nymphs and larvae to their own dwelling. When the young are born, they will work for and feed their captors.

From time to time Amazon ants repeat these attacks on other nests to capture more workers and replace those who die.

When the young queen has to create a new colony, she looks for a nest inhabited by another species and enters it. If its inhabitants accept her, she may even replace the former queen.

HEAD OF AN
AMAZON ANT

Above: Head of an Amazon ant. Its large jaws lack bottom teeth.

Below: A group of Amazon ants stealing cocoons from an anthill. They carry them in their wide-open jaws so as not to hurt them.

Right: Anthill of Amazon ants, where the "slave" workers can be seen ① looking after the larvae, and ② moving cocoons.

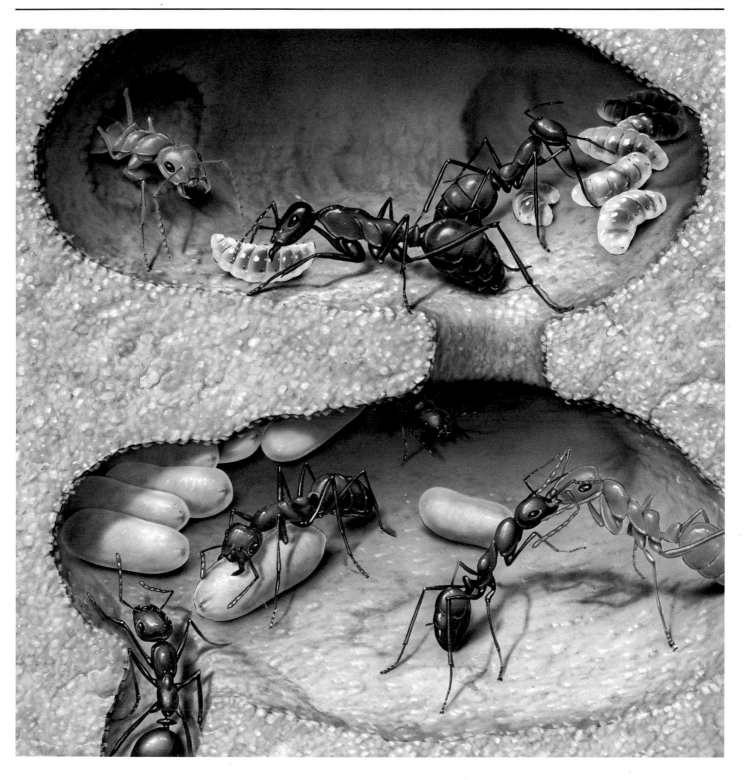

FOOD

Ants are **omnivorous**, which means that they feed on both animals and plants, although often they prefer a particular kind of food.

Some of them are hunters that capture a great number of insects' larvae and other tiny animals. Sometimes the prey is much larger than the ants and several workers are needed to carry it to the nest. They may also tear it into little pieces.

Other species prefer the seeds of certain plants, such as wheat. They gather up many grains and store them in chambers they use as granaries. When they are in the nest, they crush the seeds and mix them with saliva until they form a mush called **"ants' bread,"** which feeds all the colony.

Among the honey ants there is a special breed of workers called **bottle workers** that hang by their legs from the ceiling in special chambers. In their abdomens, which expand, they store sugared liquids carried to them by their companions. This serves as food for the rest of the community to consume as needed.

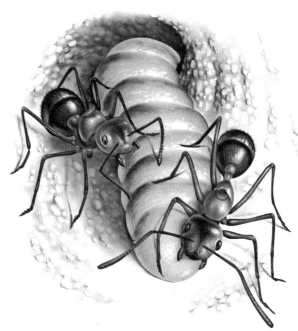

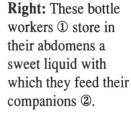

Right: These bottle workers ① store in their abdomens a sweet liquid with which they feed their companions ②.

Above: Hunter ants drag a caterpillar inside the anthill.

Below: (A) Soldier carrying a wheat grain to its anthill. (B) Peeling the grain. (C) Soldier and worker chewing the grain to make "ants' bread."

A   B   C

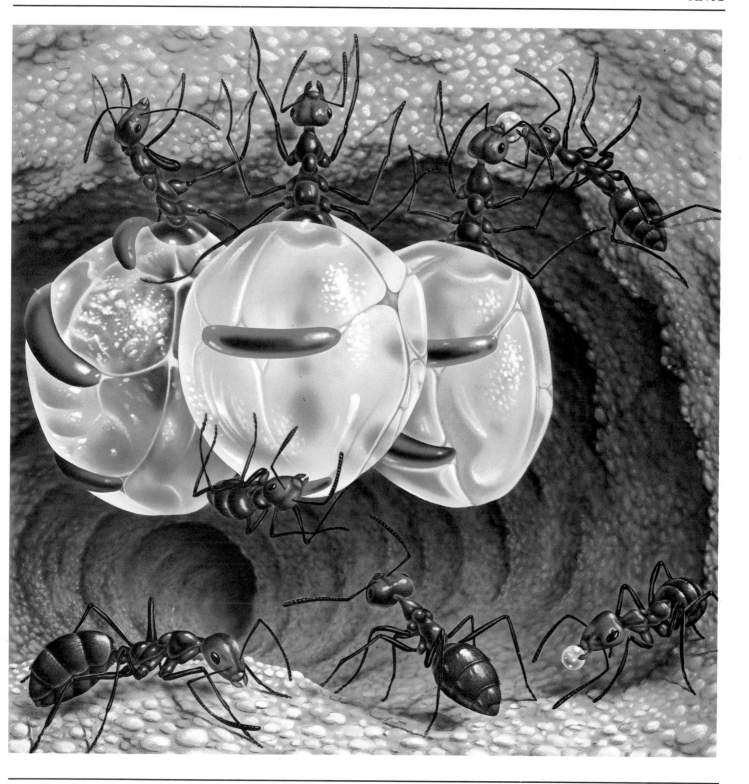

FARMERS AND STOCK FARMERS

Most ants are fond of sweet juices from plants and fruits. Some ants feed on the "honeydew" made by aphids.

The workers touch the abdomens of these little insects with their antennae and the aphids release drops of honeydew that the ants lick eagerly. In turn, they protect the aphids from their enemies.

In a similar way, ants carry the larvae of certain butterflies to their nests and feed on the juices that these larvae produce. In turn, the larvae feed on the ants' young. This relationship, in which both parties benefit, is called **symbiosis**.

There are some species of ants, such as the South American leaf-cutting ant, that grow fungi. Workers cut the leaves of trees with their powerful jaws and take them to their large underground nests. In the anthill there are large chambers where the smallest workers chew the leaves and prepare a paste upon which the fungi that they live on grow.

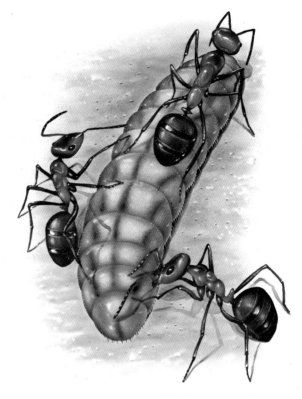

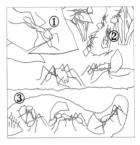

Right: Leaf-cutting ants chewing pieces of leaves ① and carrying them to the anthill ②. They carry the small pieces in their jaws and the larger pieces over their heads. Inside the anthill, the workers prepare paste for growing fungi ③.

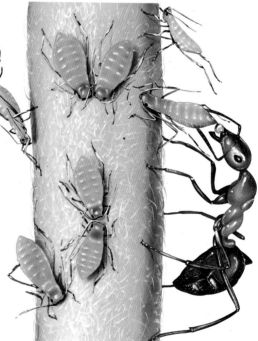

Above: Ants feeding on the juices secreted by the caterpillar they have carried into the anthill.

Right: An ant licks a drop of honeydew that an aphid has secreted when the ant's antennae have stroked its abdomen.

GREAT TRAVELERS

When food becomes scarce, some species of ants migrate; that is, they leave their anthill and go to some other place. However, no migration can compare to that of the *army ants*.

They live in Africa and South America, but their anthills are temporary. The colony finds some natural cavity and remains there while the queen lays a large number of eggs. Some time later they leave, carrying the young.

As thousands of ants march in row after row, they capture any prey they find on their way: insect larvae, spiders, grasshoppers, and even small animals.

In the center of the marching ants are the queen and the small workers that carry the larvae. Around them are a great number of workers, somewhat larger, which protect them, while the soldiers, which are even larger, are on the outer edges.

Every day they camp in a different place, gathering around the queen. The following day they begin the march again.

Some weeks later, they move into a new shelter that will serve as a nest until their next migration.

Right: Everything is ready to protect the queen ① and the larvae ②, which are carried by the small workers. The small workers are flanked by the larger workers ③ ④ and the soldiers ⑤.

NOMAD (WANDERING) STAGE   SEDENDARY (NESTING) STAGE   NOMAD STAGE

ENEMIES, LARGE AND SMALL

A nts have many enemies: birds, like **woodpeckers**, **lizards**, **frogs**, and **toads**. Some **beetles** go into the anthill to eat the larvae and nymphs. Outside, there is also danger: many ants are caught in spiders' webs. There are also some mammals that like ants. The **chimpanzee**, "fishes" them with a stick, and the **anteater** destroys anthills with its claws and captures the ants with its long and sticky tongue.

When danger threatens them ants give off chemical alarm signals and the workers rush to protect the colony.

They are not completely defenseless however, because they can bit their enemies with their jaws. Some species also have a venomous sting, like that of bees,

that they use either for defense or to attack their prey. Some ants do not have a sting but have a venom bag from which they can spray small drops of irritating fluid.

Right: Ants attack and defend themselves in different ways: (A) Biting with their strong jaws. (B) Spraying poisonous drops. (C) Introducing poison with their sting.

Right: In tropical South America the anteater is the most dangerous of the ants' enemies. Its long, sticky tongue can reach the deepest areas of the anthill, capturing larvae, nymphs, and adults, and damaging everything else despite the chemical alarm signals emitted along all the tunnels.

26

ANTS AND MAN

Ants can cause serious damage. Some of them, such as the *carpenter ant*, attack healthy wood, making tunnels in trees. Other ants enter houses, ruin food, and become general nuisances.

In tropical countries, farmers fight the *leaf-cutting ant* that strips leaves off plants in order to cultivate its fungi, thereby damaging the farms. But we can also profit from ants: In South America, people eat roasted ants, and in many countries "ant eggs" are sold commercially as food for fish and birds. The *red ant*, often found in European forests, is very useful because it fights against certain other insects. Every day these diligent ants capture thousands of insects that people consider harmful.

Right: The industrious red ants help humans in their fight against certain other insects. Every day workers and soldiers capture caterpillars ①, beetles ②, and even large insects, preventing them from invading the fields and damaging the crops.

Left: (A) Tobacco plant with its large leaves completely ruined by the devastating action of the leaf-cutting ant. (B) Cross section of a tree trunk where the tunnels dug by the carpenter ant can be seen.

A. TOBACCO PLANT DAMAGED BY THE LEAF-CUTTING ANT

B. TUNNELS DUG BY THE CARPENTER ANT

Glossary

abdomen. Rear part of the body behind the thorax.

Amazon ant. Ant that is not capable of obtaining its own food; it captures other ants and forces them to gather its food.

"ant eggs." Nymphs of ants encased in their cocoons.

antenna. Organ of sensation located on the head of the ant.

"ants' bread." Mush formed by crushing seeds and mixing them with saliva; this product feeds the entire colony.

army ants. Ants that periodically migrate great distances to establish new nesting sites.

bottle worker. Ant that hangs by its legs from the ceiling of the anthill; sugared liquids carried to it by other ants are stored in its abdomen.

carpenter ant. Ant that makes tunnels in old tree trunks by chewing the wood with its jaws.

cocoon. Silk covering enveloping the nymphs of certain ants to protect them.

colony. A community of ants belonging to the same species and living together.

Hymenoptera. Order of insects whose head, thorax, and abdomen are clearly differentiated. It includes ants, bees, and wasps.

larva. A phase in the metamorphosis or development of an ant from egg to adult.

leaf-cutting ant. Ant that strips leaves off plants.

metamorphosis. Complete transformation of the body of an ant during its development.

migration. Movement of ants from one place to another.

nomad stage. Wandering phase of the legionary ant.

nymph. Juvenile stage in the development of an ant.

omnivorous. Animal that eats vegetables as well as other animals.

peduncle. Joint between the thorax and the abdomen.

prey. Animal captured by ants to feed on it.

queen. The reproductive female ant that lays eggs and produces descendants.

red ant. Ant that kills and eats certain other insects.

sedentary stage. Nesting phase of the legionary ant.

soldier. Worker of large size and with powerful jaws whose task is defending the colony.

spinner ant. Ant that constructs nests by connecting one tree leaf to another with silk threads woven by its larvae.

symbiosis. Partnership between two different species that is of mutual benefit.

thorax. Central part of the body of the ant with six legs attached to it.

workers. Sterile female ants, incapable of laying eggs.

Index

Boldface numbers indicate illustrations